IN THE DOGHOUSE...

That's where all the fun is with that delightful dog, Marmaduke. The best friend of man, woman, and child alike, the big ham with a heart of gold is sure to brighten your day with his canine capers. So join in the laughter 'cause there's never a dull moment with

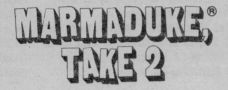

More Big Laughs from SIGNET

MARMADUKE, TAKE 2

BRAD ANDERSON

A SIGNET BOOK

NEW AMERICAN LIBRARY

SIGNET TRADEMARK REG. U.S. PAT. OFF. AND FOREIGN COUNTRIES
REGISTERED TRADEMARK—MARCA REGISTRADA
HECHO EN CHICAGO, U.S.A.

SIGNET, SIGNET CLASSIC, MENTOR, PLUME, MERIDIAN AND
NAL BOOKS are published by New American Library,
1633 Broadway, New York, New York 10019

First Printing, December, 1984

1 2 3 4 5 6 7 8 9

"Marmaduke...I don't need any
Monday morning sympathy!"

1-3-83

© 1982 United Feature Syndicate, Inc.

© 1982 United Feature Syndicate, Inc.

1-4-83

BRAD ANDERSON

"Stop trying to hypnotize me into
giving up my chair!"

BRAD ANDERSON

"He gets so jealous when we watch
that cat program!"

"How did he ever get into the car pool?"

"This is *not* my idea of cozy!"

1·7·83   © 1982 United Feature Syndicate, Inc.

"Take your bone back. I don't
take bribes!"

1-10 © 1983 United Feature Syndicate, Inc.

BRAD ANDERSON

"What he needs is a muzzle for his tail!"

"...He doesn't like the same programs we do!"

1-12 © 1983 United Feature Syndicate, Inc.

"We *could* have your dog license revoked, you know!"

"All I know is, he was chasing a squirrel..."

"Mom! He's fluffing the couch again!"

"Marmaduke loves that dog food. It's a
200-wag dinner!"

© 1983 United Feature Syndicate, Inc.

1-17

"From now on, have the paperboy drop off *two* newspapers!"

"What other game do you know?"

"Dad should never have let Marmaduke
take the lead!"

"What's this about you talking back to him?"

© 1983 United Feature Syndicate, Inc.

"I once made the mistake of giving him
some scraps from my lunch!"

© 1983 United Feature Syndicate, Inc.

"Really...you and your scary
cartoon shows!"

"Instead of 'sic 'em,' we just say,
'sit on 'em!'"

"He's the only dog I know that can sleep with one eye open for cats."

"He's guilty about something...and I'm
afraid to find out what it is."

"I'd be willing to pay *you* not to bring him in here again."

1-28

"But it's a real bargain!"

"I said, have a drink...not a shower!"

"And now, with an opposing viewpoint on
the new leash law..."

"Marmaduke's not making toast...he's just
warming his ears and nose!"

"Come on down, Marmaduke...we have to
practice taking off bandages, too!"

"A police car in our backyard. Marmaduke,
you sure can ruin my day!"

"That was a short walk...just
thirty seconds!"

"All in favor of a pizza, raise your hand!"

"They want you to be their mascot."

"Nope! Your rubber ball isn't under
that chair!"

"Yep! Marmaduke's there to greet
me...don't stop the bus until I get my knee
pads, elbow pads and helmet adjusted!"

"I can't believe this! I just had all the
wheels balanced!"

2-11   © 1983 United Feature Syndicate, Inc.

"Will you hold this a moment, sir, while I tie
my shoe?"

© 1983 United Feature Syndicate, Inc.

"Oh, no, you don't! We're not having any
live-ins here!"

"Cross your heart! I'm not receiving
stolen goods!"

2-14

BRAD ANDERSON

"Don't you ever have afternoon dates?"

"It's uncanny the way he heads for the refrigerator when he walks in his sleep!"

"You're our patient, Marmaduke, and you
have to wait an hour before we
can see you."

"I think he's in love again."

"I see you edging back over here again...but you're not coming up here on the couch!"

"I don't know what's so awful about getting
your feet wet!"

"The money wasted on obedience schools
cannot be taken as a tax loss!"

BRAD ANDERSON

"When his tail wags like that, he's gloating over some mischief he's gotten away with!"

"No! I'm not going to turn up the heat!"

"He's been suspiciously well-behaved
all day!"

"Go keep somebody else company!"

"I'll be glad when winter is over and he
goes back to sleeping in his doghouse!"

"We have our own insect control...
Marmaduke barks at the house and they
all disappear!"

3-2

© 1983 United Feature Syndicate, Inc.

"Hurry up! I have to brush my teeth!"

"Gee! I never have any problem collecting
on my paper route!"

"I didn't bring him. I thought you did!"

"Some reputation...now they won't even let you enroll!"

VET

3-7   © 1983 United Feature Syndicate, Inc.

"But, doctor...your vacation doesn't start
until tomorrow!"

"Who would think *we* would ever have
an energy crisis?"

3-9

"Nothing much...just an elephant missing
from the circus!"

"Couldn't you wait until I get home to let
me know you got into trouble today?"

3-11   © 1983 United Feature Syndicate, Inc.   BRAD ANDERSON

"You *can't* help...it's against union rules!"

"You mean, *he* has to approve
before you buy?"

"I let him carry my books, but
never my lunch."

3-15

"He's been more normal than
usual today!"

"This is for the head of the house...er...let
me rephrase that!"

© 1983 United Feature Syndicate, Inc.

3-16

"There must be *something* about you
that's deductible!"

"I'm glad he's *your* best friend!"

"I saw Marmaduke barking at it!"

"Now...Marmaduke!"

"He heard me mention spring cleaning!"

"I'm sorry, but when we have guests,
Marmaduke thinks he's on the
entertainment committee!"

"What did *you* do to get in the
doghouse...if you'll forgive
the expression?"

© 1983 United Feature Syndicate, Inc.

3-25

"Aren't you going to stand while they play
the National Anthem, Pop?"

"Now, look...I don't need *two* copilots!"

"Phil, you'd better get up!"

© 1983 United Feature Syndicate, Inc.

3-29

"He's after the 'hubcap hijacker' and has a
warrant to search your doghouse!"

"They're not *my* cold feet."

"May I?"

© 1983 United Feature Syndicate, Inc.

"Don't let him in! Don't let him in!"

4-2

"Mr. Snyder warned Marmaduke to stay
out of his yard, or he'll break every bone in
Marmaduke's doghouse."

4-4 © 1983 United Feature Syndicate, Inc.

"Of course he's not hungry...he's already eaten my slippers, pipe and newspaper!"

© 1983 United Feature Syndicate, Inc.

"What a waste of money it was buying
them each a jogging suit!"

"You call *that* the pitter-patter
of little feet?"

"He isn't very subtle, is he?"

"No, he's not attack trained, he's
friendly trained!"

"Hold the steaks...I'm waiting for him to steal my old shoe!"

"You can just forget the tip."

"This dog training manual sounds good,
execpt for the part about hypnotizing him!"

4-13   BRAD ANDERSON

"Remember, Marmaduke...tell him when I
say *no*, I mean *no*!"

"She caught him running around with a
French poodle!"

"I refuse to tell her you're not home! If you
are breaking up, tell her yourself!"

"All week, you want to go for a walk at
10 a.m., but Saturday you want to
go at 5 a.m.!"

"What are we gonna tell the boss?
Instead of picking him up, we got chased
out of town."

"Can we borrow your TV until
ours is fixed?"

© 1983 United Feature Syndicate, Inc.

4.20

"Don't tell me...let me guess...you took
Marmaduke to the vet."

4·21 © 1983 United Feature Syndicate, Inc.

"It's the dog show about the loving
cup you *borrowed*!"

© 1983 United Feature Syndicate, Inc.

4-22

"If there's one thing I can't stand, it's a
male chauvinist backseat driver."

4·23   © 1983 United Feature Syndicate, Inc.

"Who gave you permission to put your
bones in with my roast?"

4.25

© 1983 United Feature Syndicate, Inc.

"I can always tell when you've been up in
the attic with the kids!"

"That was *my* bubble gum!"

4·26

"Run away from home! Join the foreign
legion! I just got this place SPOTLESS!"

"Be fair...when I have the chair, let me have *all* of it!"

"It's too bad they can't teach him to
just *blow* kisses!"

"Marmaduke! You're *embarrassing* me!"

"Do you think the world has gone to the *people*? What am I saying?"

"The only good thing about this is that
I won't toss and turn all night."

"I don't care how he got it, as long as
he has a chair of his own!"

"If he's waiting for an invitation to dinner,
he has a long wait!"

"It's hard to train him since he already
knows how *not to* obey!"

"Let's clean up before the Environmental
Protection Agency gets involved!"

"Marmaduke better get in shape. He let the
season's first ice cream truck get away!"

5-11 © 1983 United Feature Syndicate, Inc.

"When I yell for somebody to answer the phone, I don't mean *you*!"

"Oh, you've never met Marmaduke's pet frog, have you?"

5·12

"It's bad enough sleeping with you, but do
you have to talk in your sleep, too?"

"An emergency has just arisen...can I call you back?"

"Catch it--catch that fly!"

5-16   © 1983 United Feature Syndicate, Inc.

"It could be worse...what if he didn't
like us?"

"No! I can't play 'fetch' now!"

"We're in Marmaduke's territory. I'm
surprised he isn't chasing us."

"Who invited you to afternoon tea?"

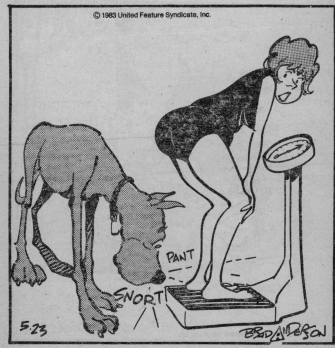

"Don't you dare breathe on that scale!
I need every break I can get!"

"How come he's *your* dog when he brings you the paper, but he's *my* dog when he wants to go out?!"

"Since when does he need all his toys when we go for a ride?"

5·26

"I don't like how springtime affects
him, either!"

"Dottie! Do we have anything to snack on
besides bones and dog food?"